This book belongs to:

Printed in Great Britain
by Amazon

62855461R00066